Dinosaur Discovery

ANKYLOSAURUS

GAIL RADLEY

BLACK
RABBIT
BOOKS

Bolt is published by Black Rabbit Books
P.O. Box 3263, Mankato, Minnesota, 56002.
www.blackrabbitbooks.com
Copyright © 2021 Black Rabbit Books

Marysa Storm, editor; Catherine Cates, interior
designer; Michael Sellner, cover designer;
Omay Ayres, photo researcher

Library of Congress Cataloging-in-Publication Data
Names: Radley, Gail, author.
Title: Ankylosaurus / Gail Radley.
Description: Mankato, Minnesota : Black Rabbit Books, [2021] | Series: Bolt.
dinosaur discovery | Includes bibliographical references and index. |
Audience: Ages 8-12 | Audience: Grades 4-6 | Summary: "Learn all about
Ankylosaurus through diagrams, graphs, powerful illustrations, and fun text"–
Provided by publisher.
Identifiers: LCCN 2019031874 (print) | LCCN 2019031875 (ebook) |
ISBN 9781623102449 (hardcover) | ISBN 9781644663400 (paperback) |
ISBN 9781623103385 (ebook)
Subjects: LCSH: Ankylosaurus–Juvenile literature.
Classification: LCC QE862.O65 R35 2021 (print) | LCC QE862.O65 (ebook) |
DDC 567.915-dc23
LC record available at https://lccn.loc.gov/2019031874
LC ebook record available at https://lccn.loc.gov/2019031875

Printed in the United States. 2/20

Image Credits

CONTENTS

CHAPTER 1

Meet the

ANKYLOSAURUS

An Ankylosaurus nibbles some bushes. Suddenly, a young and hungry Tyrannosaurus rex races toward it. The meat eater towers above the Ankylosaurus. But it struggles to bite the Ankylosaurus' wide, armored body! The plant eater tucks its head in. It swings its hammer tail, hitting the T. rex. The T. rex **staggers** in pain. It backs away to find an easier meal.

Ankylosaurus means "fused lizard."

Like a Tank

Ankylosaurus was a tough dinosaur for **predators** to attack. Its body was like a tank. Large bony plates covered its back. The plates had spikes and knobs. They were like an alligator's bumps but much bigger. Scientists believe even the dino's eyelids were armored. Its tail ended in a mighty club.

Long and Heavy

Ankylosaurus was only 5½ feet (1.7 meters) tall. But the dinosaur was about 5 feet (1.5 m) wide. It could be up to 33 feet (10 m) long. That's almost as long as some telephone poles. The dinosaur weighed up to 8,000 pounds (3,629 kilograms).

How Big Was Ankylosaurus? • • • • • • •

LENGTH
22 to 33
FEET
(7 to 10 m)

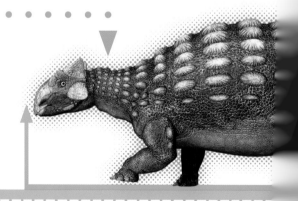

WEIGHT
about
6,000 TO 8,000 POUNDS
(2,722 to 3,629 kg)

5,000
4,000   6,000
3,000   7,000
2,000   8,000
1,000   9,000
0   10,000
pounds   pounds

PARTS OF AN ANKYLOSAURUS

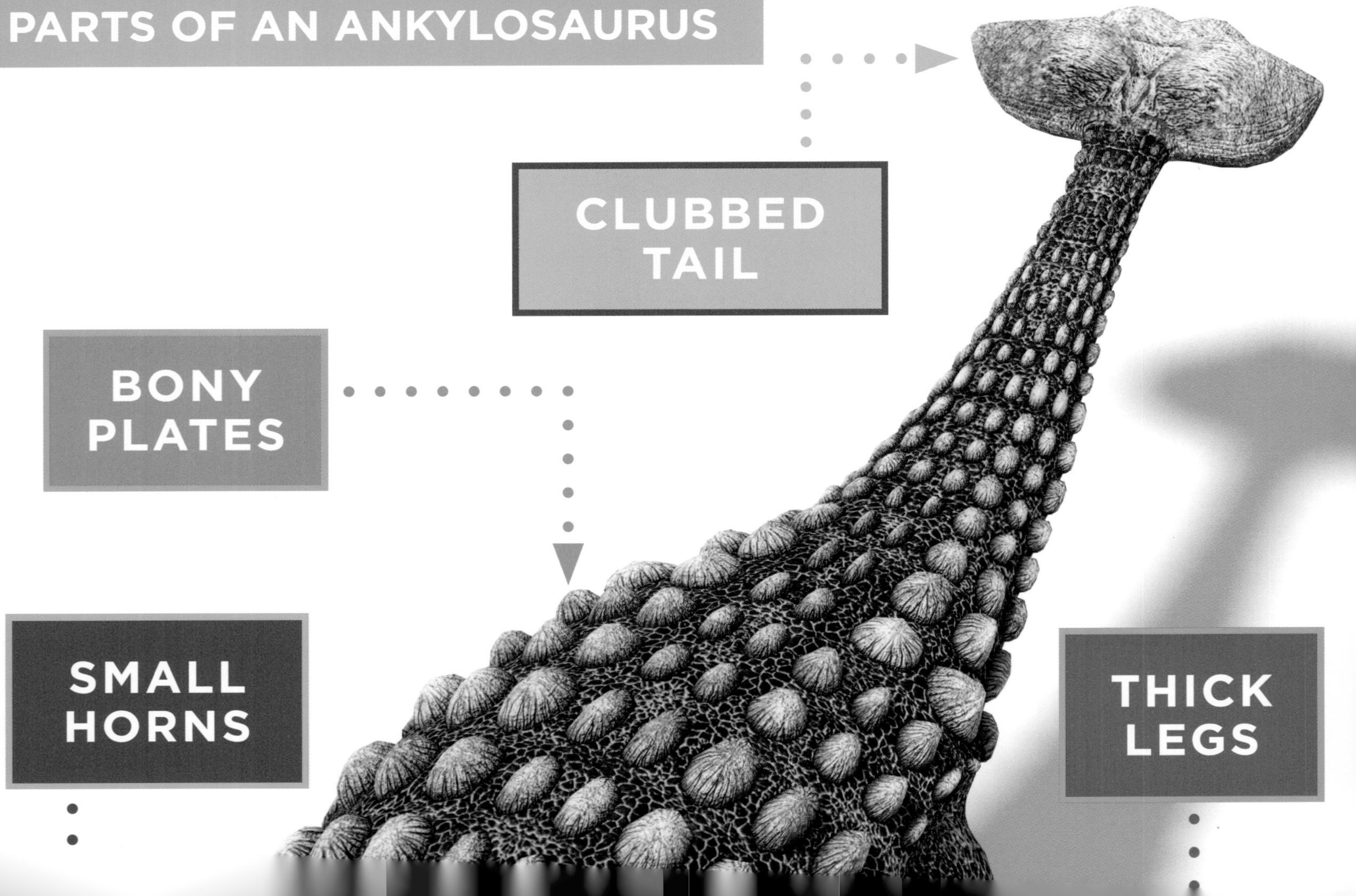

THICK LEGS

CLUBBED TAIL

BONY PLATES

SMALL HORNS

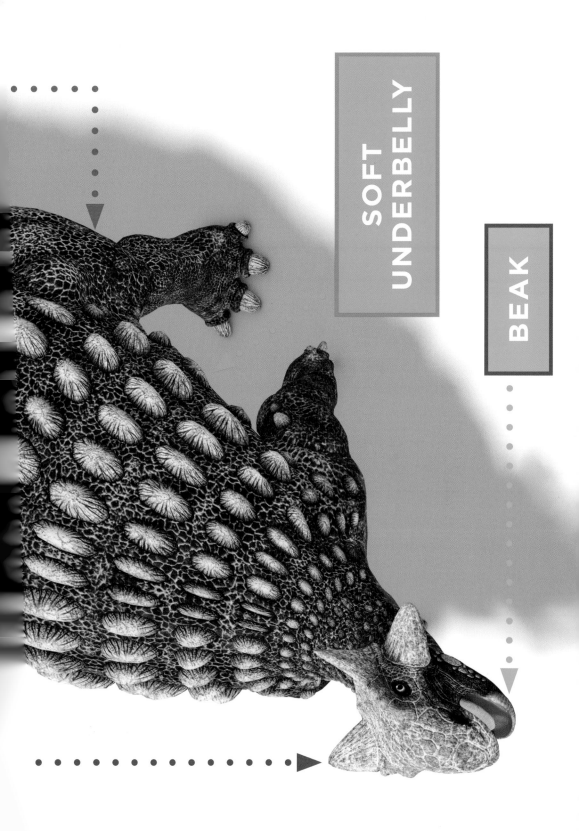

SOFT
UNDERBELLY

BEAK

Traveling Together

Scientists don't know much about dinosaur behavior. Many of today's plant eaters travel in groups, though. Scientists think plant-eating dinosaurs probably did too.

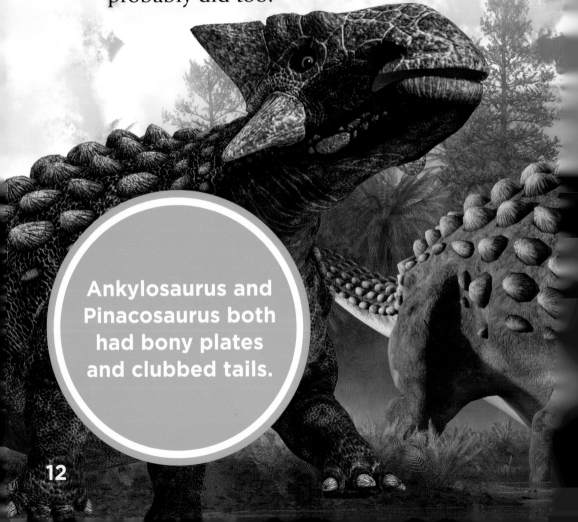

Ankylosaurus and Pinacosaurus both had bony plates and clubbed tails.

In 1969, scientists found a big group of Pinacosaurus **fossils**. The dinosaurs belong to the same family as Ankylosaurus. This finding supports the idea that Ankylosaurus traveled in groups.

CHAPTER 2

Where and
WHEN THEY LIVED

This huge dinosaur stomped around what's now western North America. That's where people have found its bones. Few Ankylosaurus fossils have ever been found, though. Scientists have only discovered three major skeletons. None were complete.

In 1906, Barnum Brown dug up the first Ankylosaurus bones. He found them in Montana.

15

Ankylosaurus was one of the last dinosaurs on Earth. People aren't sure why they disappeared. An **asteroid** or volcano might have wiped them out.

When They Lived

Ankylosaurus lived about 70 to 66 million years ago. This time was during the Late Cretaceous Age. The first **mammals**, snakes, and insects **developed** then. Dinosaurs would've walked around **ferns** and flowering plants too.

WHEN THEY LIVED

CRETACEOUS AGE
about 145 to 65 million
years ago

MILLION YEARS AGO	160	140	120

TYRANNOSAURUS REX LIVED

68 to 65 million
years ago

ANKYLOSAURUS LIVED

70 to 66 million
years ago

**DINOSAURS
DIED OUT**
about 65 million
years ago

100 **80** **60**

CHAPTER 3

WHAT THEY ATE

Since Ankylosaurus was so short, it could only reach low-lying plants. It used its beak and small teeth to pluck leaves. Scientists think the beak let the dinosaur be a picky eater. It could easily avoid certain plants. They also think the dinosaur didn't chew its food. The dinosaur didn't have any grinding teeth. It probably just took big gulps. Its stomach would do the rest.

Digging for Food

Ankylosaurus mostly ate plants. But its teeth and beak shape suggest it might have dug for worms and insects too. Scientists think the dinosaur might have even dug for roots.

What Scientists Believe
Ankylosaurus Ate

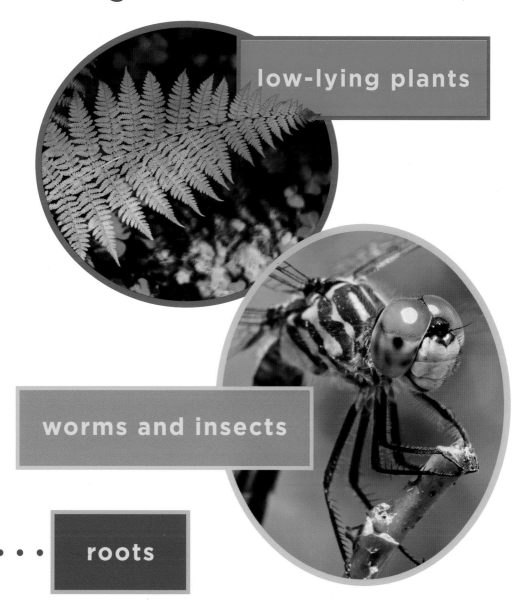

low-lying plants

worms and insects

· · · roots

People found the new bones in Montana.

CHAPTER 4

New DISCOVERIES

People are still learning about dinosaurs. In 2014, people looking for fossils found the skeleton of a new Ankylosaurus relative. It's about 75 million years old. Fossils are often scattered. But this skeleton was nearly complete. It had some armor plates still in place too. Scientists could see how they fit together. This information gave them a better picture of Ankylosaurus.

MONTANA

Wondering

Scientists have discovered a lot about Ankylosaurus. But they still have many questions about the armored dinosaur. They wonder how its body worked. They hope to know exactly what it ate and where it lived too. People keep looking for answers.

asteroid (AS-tuh-royd)—a large space rock that moves around the sun

develop (dih-VEL-uhp)—to begin to exist

fern (FURN)—a type of plant that has large, delicate leaves and no flowers

fossil (FAH-sul)—the remains or traces of plants and animals that are preserved as rock

fused (FYOOZD)—to be united by being or as if melted together

mammal (MAH-muhl)—a type of animal that feeds milk to its young and usually has hair or fur

predator (PRED-uh-tuhr)—an animal that eats other animals

stagger (STAG-er)—to move unsteadily from side to side

BOOKS

Pimentel, Annette Bay. *Do You Really Want to Meet Ankylosaurus?* Do You Really Want to Meet a Dinosaur? Mankato, MN: Amicus Illustrated and Amicus Ink, 2020.

Sabelko, Rebecca. *Ankylosaurus.* The World of Dinosaurs. Minneapolis: Bellwether Media, Inc., 2020.

Weakland, Mark. *Armored Dinosaurs: Ranking Their Speed, Strength, and Smarts.* Dinosaurs by Design. Mankato, MN: Black Rabbit Books, 2020.

WEBSITES

4 Dinosaurs that Called Canada Home
www.cbc.ca/kidscbc2/the-feed/5-dinosaurs-that-called-canada-home

Ankylosaurus
kids.nationalgeographic.com/animals/prehistoric-animals/ankylosaurus/

Ankylosaurus Facts for Kids
www.dkfindout.com/us/dinosaurs-and-prehistoric-life/dinosaurs/ankylosaurus/

INDEX